NATIVE AMERICANS OF THE WEST

A SOURCEBOOK ON THE AMERICAN WEST

NATIVE
AMERICANS
OF THE WEST

A SOURCEBOOK ON THE AMERICAN WEST

Edited by Carter Smith

AMERICAN ALBUMS FROM THE COLLECTIONS OF
THE LIBRARY OF CONGRESS

THE MILLBROOK PRESS, *Brookfield, Connecticut*

Cover: "Pehriska–Ruhpa, in the Costume of the Dog Dance." Lithograph based on a painting by Carl Bodmer, 1834.

Title Page: "Encampment of Piekann Indians near Fort McKenzie on the Musselshell River." Lithograph by Rice & Clark, 1842, based on a painting by Carl Bodmer.

Contents Page: "Indian Utensils and Arms." Lithograph based on a painting by Carl Bodmer, 1834.

Back Cover: "The Snow Shoe Dance." Lithograph by Currier & Ives, based on a painting by George Catlin, 1844.

Library of Congress Cataloging-in-Publication Data

Native Americans of the West : a sourcebook on the American West /
    edited by Carter Smith.
        p.   cm. -- (American albums from the collections of the
    Library of Congress)
        Includes bibliographical references and index.
        Summary: Describes and illustrates the Native Americans of
    the West, from before the arrival of Europeans to the Wounded
    Knee massacre in 1890, through a variety of images created
    during that period.
        ISBN 1-56294-131-3 [lib. bdg.]
        1. Indians of North America--West (U.S.)--Social life and
    customs--Juvenile literature. 2. Indians of North America--West
    (U.S.)--History--Juvenile literature. 3. Indians of North America--
    West (U.S.)--Wars--Juvenile literature. [1. Indians of North
    America--West (U.S.)--History--Sources.] I. Smith, C. Carter. II.
    Series.
    E78.W5N38 1991
    978'.00497--dc20   91-31128
                                                              CIP
                                                               AC

 Created in association with Media Projects Incorporated

C. Carter Smith, *Executive Editor*
Lelia Wardwell, *Managing Editor*
Elizabeth Prince, *Manuscript Editor*
Lisa Mirabile, *Principal Writer*
Charles A. Wills, *Consulting Editor, Writer*
Kimberly Horstman, *Researcher*
Lydia Link, *Designer*
Athena Angelos, *Photo Researcher*

The consultation of Bernard F. Reilly, Jr., Head Curator of the
Prints and Photographs Division of the Library of Congress, is
gratefully acknowledged.

Contents

Most nineteenth-century depictions of Indians by white artists presented one of the two extremes: They were shown either as cruel savages or, as in this lithograph, fierce but noble warriors.

Introduction

NATIVE AMERICANS OF THE WEST is one of the volumes in a series published by The Millbrook Press titled AMERICAN ALBUMS FROM THE COLLECTIONS OF THE LIBRARY OF CONGRESS and one of six books in the series subtitled SOURCEBOOKS ON THE AMERICAN WEST. This series treats the history of the West from pioneer days to the early twentieth century.

The editors' goal for the series is to make available to the student many of the original visual documents of the American past that are preserved in the Library of Congress. Featured prominently in NATIVE AMERICANS OF THE WEST are the rich holdings of the Prints and Photographs Division, and some of the thousands of illustrated books and magazines in the Library's general collections. The volume includes many of the lithographed portraits of Native Americans produced by early nineteenth-century artists such as George Catlin, Carl Bodmer, and Charles Bird King, who painted the portrait of Chief Black Hawk. These images were usually accurate and relatively objective. Less believable, however, are the portrayals of battles and encounters with Indians that appeared in the form of popular prints and magazine illustrations both before and after the Civil War. These illustrations tended to romanticize events, and to exaggerate the threat posed by Native Americans. By the late nineteenth century, nearly all American Indian tribes were confined to reservations, having been forced to surrender their claims to Western territory. (It is interesting to compare the ferocious and powerful Indians in Remington's works with the much less imposing figures in photographs of the same period.)

These pictorial records, then, are as important for what they show as for how they show it. Being almost without exception documents created by white Americans for an audience of other whites, the works reproduced here offer a wealth of insight into the Easterners' perceptions of the Native Americans. Sadly, we are left with little of the Indian civilizations' own records of their lives and achievements. Such as they are, the works reproduced here are part of the rich record of Western life preserved by the Library of Congress in its role as the nation's library.

BERNARD F. REILLY, JR.

During the Revolutionary War, some Indians were British allies, and some joined the American side. In 1789, one of the first acts of the new U.S. Congress established the Appalachian Mountains as a border between Indians and settlers. The same law guaranteed Indian lands. Nevertheless, pioneers continued to cross into Indian Territory. Through treaties and warfare, the Indians were pushed steadily westward.

The Louisiana Purchase in 1803 doubled the area of the United States. After 1815, the government decided to move Indians to reservations beyond the Mississippi River. In an 1838 incident known as the Trail of Tears, the entire Cherokee tribe was marched from Georgia to Oklahoma. The California Gold Rush increased Indian contact with settlers, and epidemics devastated Indian populations. Demand accelerated for Indian lands. As Indians resisted, warfare ensued, becoming especially fierce after the Civil War.

In 1887, Congress passed the General Allotment Act, or Dawes Act, which parceled out communal reservations to individual Indians. The Indians gave over much territory. While drafted to make Indians individual property owners, the Dawes Act ultimately broke up Indian communities, and impoverished those who had survived wars, migrations, and epidemics.

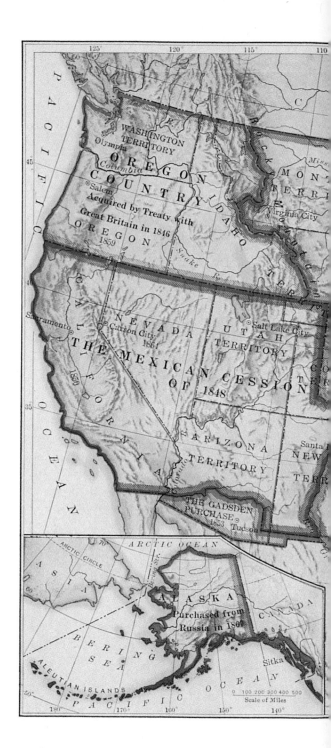

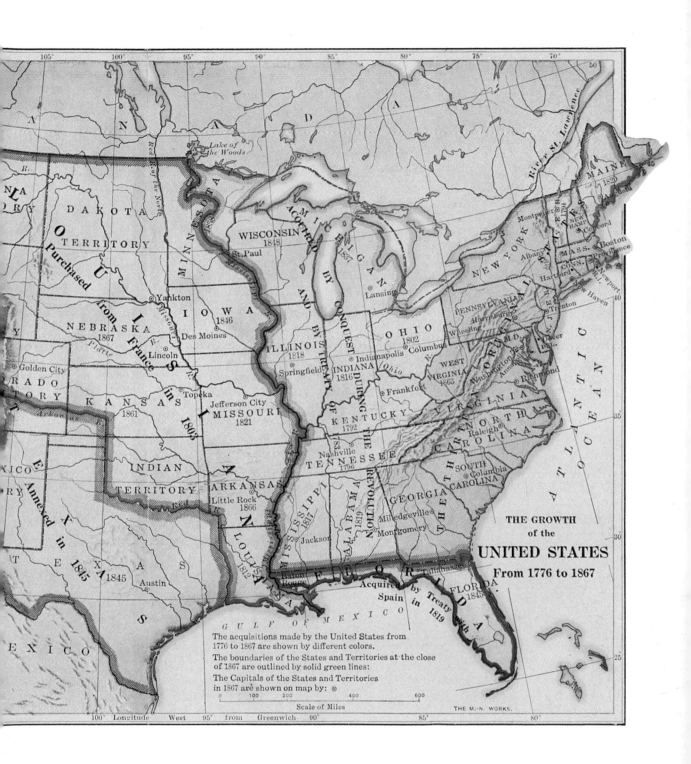

THE GROWTH
of the
UNITED STATES
From 1776 to 1867

The acquisitions made by the United States from 1776 to 1867 are shown by different colors.

The boundaries of the States and Territories at the close of 1867 are outlined by solid green lines:

The Capitals of the States and Territories in 1867 are shown on map by: ⊙

0   100   200   400   600

Scale of Miles

THE M: N. WORKS.

9

Born in Georgia in 1760, Sequoya, a Cherokee Indian, gave his people what most other Indian nations lacked: a written language. After a crippling accident ended his career as a hunter, Sequoya developed a system in which modified English letters represented sounds in the Cherokee language. He is shown here with some of the eighty-six symbols that made up the Cherokee alphabet.

The story of relations between the Indians who had lived in North America for thousands of years and the European immigrants who arrived after Christopher Columbus is mostly a story of conflict. Often, Indians and whites were friendly to each other, since both stood to gain from friendship. Indians taught the white settlers much about survival in their new land. In turn, whites brought many new technologies to the Indians, such as metal pots for cooking and knives for hunting.

Unfortunately, the Europeans also brought disease, especially smallpox, to which the Indians had no immunity. And they brought alcohol, which was also new to the Indians and proved to be destructive. But perhaps most important, the Europeans brought guns, which gave them a permanent technological edge over the Indians. Although the Indians themselves quickly acquired guns, they rarely had the most advanced firearms, and they remained dependent on Europeans for gunpowder and other supplies.

In the end, these unbalanced friendships almost always disintegrated into a struggle for control over the land. Since the Indians had little concept of the ownership of land, they often did not understand the full meaning of the treaties they signed. Disagreements were settled by force—conflicts that the whites usually won. By the middle of the nineteenth century, the Indians had been forced almost completely out of the eastern United States.

UNITED STATES HISTORY

1789 George Washington becomes the first president of the United States.

1791 The Bill of Rights is added to the Constitution.

1792 Thomas Jefferson forms the Republican Party to oppose the Federalists and to represent the rights of farmers and those in favor of a less centralized government.

1792 Washington and Adams are reelected president and vice president.

1793 Construction of the Capitol building begins.

1794 The U.S. and Britain sign Jay's Treaty, in which the British agree to evacuate the Great Lakes region.
•Richard Allen, a freed slave living in Philadelphia, becomes the first bishop of the newly founded African Methodist Episcopal Church.

1796 Federalist John Adams is elected president and Democratic-Republican Thomas Jefferson is elected vice president.

1797 Adams is inaugurated as the the country's second president.

1798 Congress repeals all treaties with France and orders the U.S. Navy to capture French ships.

The founders of the first African Methodist Episcopal Church

NATIVE AMERICANS OF THE WEST

1789 The Wyandot, Delaware, Potawatomi, Ottawa, and Sauk tribes agree to give land in the Northwest Territory to the U.S. in exchange for payment.
•The Cherokee Wars end with the Battle of Flint Creek when the Cherokees are defeated by white settlers.

1790 Brigadier General Josiah Harmar leads a major U.S. military campaign against the Miami Indians, destroying their crops and villages. The Indians counterattack and drive him back to Fort Washington (now Cincinnati, Ohio).

1791 A coalition of Northwest Indians, led by Miami chief Little Turtle, ambushes Governor Arthur St. Clair's army on the upper Wabash River, in Ohio. The attack leaves 630 Americans dead and 300 wounded.

1792 In response to the Indian threat in the South and the Old Northwest, Congress enlarges the army, forming the Legion of the United States. General Anthony Wayne is selected as commander.

1794 General Wayne defeats the Indian Northwest Confederation (Chippewa, Miami, Delaware, Shawnee, Potawatomi, and Cherokee tribes) in the Battle of Fallen Timbers.

1795 The Treaty of Greenville ends conflicts between the U.S. and the Indians of the Old Northwest; the Indians cede two-thirds of what is now Ohio.

Little Turtle

1799 Adams re-opens negotiations with France in an effort to avoid war.

1800 The presidential election results in a tie between Thomas Jefferson and Aaron Burr; the House of Representatives elects Jefferson president, and Burr vice president.
• The U.S. census cites the population of the nation at 5.3 million. Virginia is the most populous state.
• The Library of Congress is created.

1801 American inventor Robert Fulton builds the *Nautilus*, a human-powered submarine.
• The first suspension bridge is built at Uniontown, Pennsylvania.
• *The New York Evening Post* is published in New York City by Alexander Hamilton and John Jay.

1802 The U.S. Military Academy is established by Congress; it is located at West Point, New York, on the Hudson River.

1804 Alexander Hamilton is killed in a duel with political opponent Aaron Burr in Weehawken, New Jersey.

1806 The *Clermont* is built by Robert Fulton; it is the first commercially successful steamboat in the U.S.

1811 Construction begins on the Cumberland Road, the first major highway funded by the federal government. The road eventually runs from Cumberland, Maryland, to Vandalia, Illinois.

1812 Congress declares war on Britain on June 18.

1814 Attorney Francis Scott Key composes the famous "Star Spangled Banner" after the defeat of the British at Baltimore, Maryland.

1817 Thomas Gallaudet opens the first school in the U.S. for the deaf, the American Asylum, in Hartford, Connecticut.

A Seminole village

1803 Many Indian tribes are brought under the control of the U.S. government as a result of the Louisiana Purchase.

1804 Meriwether Lewis and William Clark begin their expedition to explore the West, accompanied by Sacajawea, a Shoshone Indian, who is their guide and interpreter.

1811 Shawnee leader Tecumseh forms a confederation of Indian tribes to resist white settlement in the Indiana Territory. His brother, Tenskwatawa, leads an unsuccessful attack on William Henry Harrison's army camp in the Battle of Tippecanoe.

1813 American forces, led by Harrison, defeat British troops and their Indian allies in the Battle of the Thames, fought in Canada during the War of 1812. Tecumseh is killed in the war.

1814 Major General Andrew Jackson defeats the Creek Indians at the Battle of Horseshoe Bend in Alabama. The battle ends the Creek War, begun in 1813 with the Indian attack on Fort Mims.

1817 The First Seminole War begins between the Seminoles of Florida and Georgia and U.S. troops under General Andrew Jackson.

UNITED STATES HISTORY

1820 The New York Stock Exchange becomes the nation's leading stock exchange.
•The fourth census of the U.S. cites the nation's population at 10 million.

1821 The first public high school in the U.S. is established in Boston, Massachusetts.

1823 President Monroe presents his Monroe Doctrine to Congress. In it he warns European nations not to interfere in the affairs of countries in the Western Hemisphere.

1824 John Quincy Adams is elected president by the U.S. House of Representatives when none of the other candidates win a majority vote in the national election.

1825 The Erie Canal is completed; it runs from Lake Erie to the Hudson River at Albany, New York.

1826 Thomas Jefferson and John Adams die on the same day—July 4, 1826.

1828 Andrew Jackson becomes the seventh president, defeating John Quincy Adams.

1834 Abraham Lincoln enters politics for the first time, joining the assembly of the Illinois legislature; he is twenty-five years old.

1835 The national debt is completely paid off as a result of revenues from increased railroad construction and skyrocketing land values.

1836 Abolitionists present anti-slavery petitions to Congress.

1837 Mount Holyoke, the first permanent women's college, is founded in Massachusetts.

1840 William Henry Harrison defeats Martin Van Buren in the presidential elections, using the

NATIVE AMERICANS OF THE WEST

1821 Sequoya invents the Cherokee alphabet, which gives the Cherokees a written version of their language.

1824 Thomas L. McKenney is appointed first head of the Bureau of Indian Affairs.

1825 Creek chief William McIntosh signs over ancestral lands to the state of Georgia in the Treaty of Indian Springs. He is killed by a squad of Creeks for breaking a tribal law forbidding Indians to sell their land to the U.S.
•U.S. government representatives meet with leaders of midwestern Indian tribes at the Council of Prairie du Chien, Wisconsin, to set boundaries for each Indian group in the area.

1830 Under the Indian Removal Act of 1830, thousands of Cherokee, Seminole, Choctaw, Creek, and Chickasaw Indians are moved from their homes in Alabama, Tennessee, Georgia, and Mississippi to Oklahoma, in what is known as the Trail of Tears. Four thousand die en route.

1832 Black Hawk's War is fought between U.S. troops and Sauk and Fox Indians over land in Illinois. Chief Black Hawk surrenders in the Battle of Bad Axe.

The meeting at Prarie du Chien

campaign slogan "Tippecanoe and Tyler, too." John Tyler is elected vice president.

1841 President Harrison dies after one month in office. John Tyler succeeds him as president.

1845 The House and the Senate adopt a joint resolution calling for the annexation of Texas. It becomes the twenty-eighth state in the Union.

1848 A coalition of antislavery groups

Cover of Uncle Tom's Cabin

forms the Free Soil Party and nominates Martin Van Buren for president.

1849 The Gold Rush begins as the first gold miners arrive in San Francisco aboard the ship *California*.

1852 *Uncle Tom's Cabin* by Harriet Beecher Stowe is published, arousing strong feelings against slavery.

1856 A proslavery group attacks Lawrence, Kansas, a center of anti-slavery movement, and kills one man. In retaliation, abolitionist John Brown kills five proslavery men at Pottawotamie Creek. The term "Bleeding Kansas" becomes a commonly used name for the territory.

1860 Abraham Lincoln defeats Stephen Douglas in the presidential election, despite his lack of support in the slave states.

1861 The U.S. Civil War begins when South Carolina's forces fire on Fort Sumter near Charleston and the Union commander quickly surrenders. Robert E. Lee resigns from the U.S. Army to fight for the Confederacy.

1835 A smallpox epidemic ravages populations of the Mandan, Hidatsa, and Arikara tribes who live along the Missouri River.
•The second Seminole War breaks out when the Seminoles of Florida refuse to migrate to Indian Territory, defying the Removal Act.

1851 At Camp Traverse de Sioux in the Minnesota Territory, the Santee Sioux agree to sell their land to the U.S. govern-

ment for $3 million.
•Thomas Fitzpatrick arranges a treaty with Plains Indian tribes at Fort Laramie, Wyoming. The Indians give land to the Western trails and promise the settlers safe passage in return for some territories and a yearly payment of $50,000 worth of supplies.
•A treaty between the U.S. and the Sisseton and Wahpeton Sioux tribes forbids the sale of liquor on Indian lands.

1855 At the Walla Walla Council, the largest meeting between Indian chiefs and U.S. officials, several Northwestern tribes agree to give 60,000 square miles of land to the U.S., for an about 3 cents an acre.

1858 Many settlers and miners move into the Cheyenne and Arapaho hunting grounds in Colorado because of the Pikes Peak Gold Rush. The Indians refuse to sell their land and move to reserva-

tions, and Governor John Evans declares war on them.
•Tensions over the influx of fur traders and missionaries into the Pacific Northwest territories erupt in the Battle of Spokane Plains.

1861 Along the Apache Pass in the Territory of New Mexico, Chiricahua Apache leader Cochise leads Apache warriors in a series of raids against white settlers and travelers.

NATIVE AMERICAN CIVILIZATIONS BEFORE THE ARRIVAL OF EUROPEANS

In the first centuries after the arrival of Europeans in North America, very little was known about the native men and women who had lived on the land for centuries.

Believing he had arrived in the East Indies, Christopher Columbus named the inhabitants he encountered there "Indians." The stories early Europeans told of the "Indians" were often wild and unfounded, just like the myths the Indians invented to explain the arrival of Europeans.

It was not until the beginning of the nineteenth century that scholarly efforts to learn about "pre-historic" Indians began. In the next two centuries, scholars studied the clues that these early civilizations left behind. Among the ruins of ancient settlements and burial sites they found tools, weapons, works of art, religious items, and the remains of buildings—even garbage dumps—that have offered valuable clues about the great Native American civilizations that flourished before the arrival of Europeans. Despite these findings, early Native American culture remains a mystery to contemporary scholars.

Early Indian cultures used man-made mounds of earth as temples or tombs. Most are small, but the snakelike "Great Serpent Mound" in Ohio stretches for almost a quarter of a mile. Archaeologists believe it was built sometime between A.D. 800 and 1300.

The medicine man—an Indian who possessed great spiritual pow-
ers, often including the ability to cure the sick—was an important
figure in many tribes. This engraving (above), modeled after a
painting by Seth Eastman, appeared in Henry R. Schoolcraft's
History, Condition, & Prospects of the Indian Tribes of North
America. It shows a medicine man of one of the Algonquian-
speaking tribes of the Great Lakes area.

This rock painting (right)—perhaps of a deity—was produced by the Chinooks, who lived along Puget Sound in the Pacific Northwest. The Chinook language was used by other tribes along the Columbia River, but the Chinooks themselves adopted the language of the Chehalis tribe when they merged with that group in the nineteenth century.

The homes of the Native Americans varied widely. Some tribes lived in simple houses made of twigs or animal hides; others, especially in the Southwest, lived in complex cliff dwellings called pueblos. Shown here (below) is the Mesa Verde pueblo in Colorado, which was discovered in 1888. Its original inhabitants had long since disappeared.

THE STRUGGLE FOR THE OLD NORTHWEST

When the American Revolution ended in 1781, the new nation had technically won control of the land from the Atlantic Ocean to the Mississippi River. But just west of the thirteen new states, beyond the Appalachian Mountains, the land still belonged to the Indians.

Military conflict between the Indians and the new nation first broke out in the Northwest Territory. It began in 1790, when U.S. General Josiah Harmar led several expeditions from Fort Washington, near the site of present-day Cincinnati, against the Miami Indians of Ohio. These expeditions were inconclusive, but the next year, a force of more than 2,700 U.S. soldiers was ambushed and decisively defeated north of Fort Washington by a group of Indians from several different tribes led by Chief Little Turtle.

The United States finally won control over the Northwest Territory in 1794, when Anthony Wayne led a force of more than 5,000 U.S. soldiers against a small, disorganized group of Indians representing all the tribes of the Northwest Territory. After the Battle of Fallen Timbers, as this encounter was called, the Indians were forced to sign the Treaty of Greenville in 1795, which granted control of the Ohio Territory to the United States.

On January 9, 1789, two major treaties were signed between the U.S. government and representatives of several Indian nations at Fort Harmar (opposite, top). The first fixed the western boundary of the six nations of the Iroquois Confederacy. In the second treaty, the Wyandot, Delaware, and other tribes confirmed an earlier agreement to permit white settlement on land they had once claimed.

During the Revolutionary War, most of the tribes on the western frontier sided with the British. In 1778, frontiersman George Rogers Clark began a campaign aimed at ending Indian raids on small American settlements along the Ohio River. Clark scored some notable victories, including one at Cahokia, in which defeated Indians offered to sacrifice two members of their tribe as a token of surrender (opposite, bottom). Clark turned the offer down.

Anthony Wayne (1745–96; above) won the nickname "Mad Anthony" after a daring attack on the British fort at Stony Point, New York, during the Revolutionary War. His proven courage led President George Washington to appoint him commander of the U.S. forces on the northwest frontier. A skilled diplomat as well as a soldier, Wayne helped negotiate the 1795 Treaty of Greenville, which brought a temporary peace to the Northwest Territory.

In the early 1790s, Indian forces in the Northwest Territory defeated expeditions led by American generals Josiah Harmar and Arthur St. Clair. In the summer of 1794, troops under General Anthony Wayne met a group of 800 Indian braves led by Little Turtle (right) along the Miami River. Wayne's men were victorious in the fierce two-hour fight (opposite), which was later known as the Battle of Fallen Timbers.

INDIANS AND THE WAR OF 1812

Although the War of 1812 was largely fought over American shipping rights on the Atlantic Ocean, much of the fighting took place in the Midwest, near Lake Michigan. The U.S. and Britain both claimed the land in this territory, since whoever controlled it also controlled the area's rich fur trade. The Indians, of course, also held a claim to the area. When war broke out between the two countries, Britain sought the Indians as allies against the Americans.

The foremost Indian leaders at this time were the great Shawnee chief Tecumseh and his brother, Tenskwatawa ("the Prophet"). Tecumseh was one of the rare Indian chiefs who understood how important it was for the different Indian tribes to remain united against their common enemy: Americans who wanted to farm the land and drive the Indians off. Tecumseh was particularly bitter after the Battle of Tippecanoe, in Indiana, where his brother had been defeated in 1811. He willingly joined the British side.

The British and the Indians were at first victorious. But in 1813 the Americans won their first major victory at the Battle of the Thames, in what is now Ontario. Not only did American forces win, but they also killed Tecumseh. With him, all hope of a united Indian defense against the Americans died.

Together with his brother Tecumseh, Tenskwatawa (1768–1837, right) urged Indians to resist white settlement and preserve their traditional way of life. Tecumseh ordered Tenskwatawa (who was more of a spiritual than a military leader) to avoid combat with white forces. Tenskwatawa ignored his brother and led his Shawnee warriors to defeat at Tippecanoe Creek.

General William Henry Harrison placed sentries around his army's camp at Tippecanoe Creek, but these soldiers were quickly overwhelmed by Tenskwatawa's Indians when they attacked just before dawn on November 7, 1811. The battle was fought hand-to-hand, as depicted in this illustration (below), until the Indians retreated at first light.

Tecumseh (1768–1813; left) was unusual among Indian leaders because he tried to unite all Indians—not just his own tribe—against the fast-approaching tide of white settlement. His enemy, General William Henry Harrison, said of him, "He is one of those uncommon geniuses which spring up occasionally to produce revolutions. . ."

This cartoon (below), published in Pennsylvania in 1812, reflects the anger Western settlers felt toward Great Britain. Many believed that British outposts in Canada provided arms and guidance to the Indians who raided American settlements on the northwest frontier. Here, Indians offer the scalps of American soldiers to a British officer who promises, "the King. . .will reward you."

Tecumseh became a brigadier general in the British army after the War of 1812 broke out. On October 5, 1813, troops under General William Henry Harrison attacked a British-Indian force, which included Tecumseh, along the Thames River in what is now Ontario, Canada. Tecumseh was killed. No one knows the exact circumstances, but legend attributes the great Indian leader's death, shown in this lithograph (below), to Colonel Richard M. Johnson.

STRUGGLES IN THE SOUTH

The Indian tribes in the Southeast were slowly but surely pushed westward to accommodate the expanding United States. The Cherokees in Virginia, the Carolinas, and Georgia had waged an important fight against the United States during the American Revolution. But even with substantial British help, the Indians had been decisively beaten by 1779.

The Creek Indians, who lived in Georgia and parts of the Mississippi Territory (now Alabama), began to resist United States territorial advances in the mid-1780s and continued to fight back for twenty years. During the War of 1812, a group of Creeks known as the Red Sticks attacked Fort Mims on the Alabama River, killing over 500 whites. The outraged residents of Tennessee, Georgia, and the Mississippi Territory launched a determined campaign against them. The showdown came in 1814 at the Battle of Horseshoe Bend, on the Tallapoosa River, where the Creeks were thoroughly defeated.

After the War of 1812, conflict between Indians and whites in the Southeast was centered in Florida, which was still owned by Spain. There the United States fought the Seminole Indians over the issue of runaway American slaves, who the Seminoles (and the Spanish) were allowing to escape into Florida. In the first Seminole War from 1818 to 1819, General Andrew Jackson (later president) led U. S. troops in the defeat of the Seminoles. As a result of the war, Spain sold Florida to the United States in 1819.

This diagram (below) outlines the position of American troops around a horseshoe-shaped bend in the Tallapoosa River. It was here, on March 27, 1814, that General Andrew Jackson's force overwhelmed the Upper Creeks in a battle that ended with about 900 Indians killed and 500 (mostly women and children) captured.

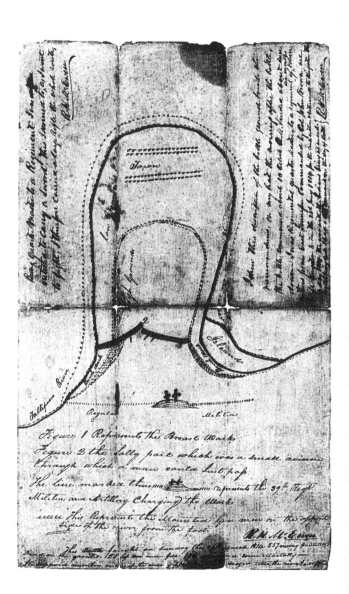

Son of a Scottish father and a Creek mother, William McIntosh (c. 1790–1825; left) was leader of the Lower Creeks—an Indian group friendly to the U.S. government. His bitter feud with Menawa, leader of the anti-American Upper Creeks, finally ended in 1825 when Menawa murdered him. The murder was approved by many Creeks, who were angered by McIntosh's decision to sell 10 million acres of Creek land to Georgia—a violation of tribal law.

This romantic but inaccurate 1845 engraving (below) shows Creek Indians attacking Fort Mims, in Alabama, on August 30, 1813. Because the fort commander failed to post sentries or even to close all of its gates, about 1,000 Creek warriors easily entered the small structure. All but 36 of the 553 whites in the fort—most of them civilians— were killed, and the fort was burned.

THE COUNCIL OF PRAIRIE DU CHIEN

Although the U. S. Congress had promised in 1789 that the Indians' "land and property shall never be taken from them without their consent," such consent often took the form of deceptive treaties that both sides frequently broke. In 1804, for example, the chiefs of the Sauk and Fox tribes of Illinois signed a treaty they thought simply allowed Americans to hunt on their land. In fact, they had given away 50 million acres.

In August of 1825, representatives of the tribes who lived in the central and northern regions around the Mississippi River gathered. This council included members of the Chippewa (also called Ojibwa), Iowa Sioux, Sauk, Fox, Menominee, and Winnebago tribes. They met in a grand council with representatives of the United States government at Prairie du Chien, Wisconsin. There, they concluded one of the first treaties between the Indians of the Midwest and the federal government.

The Council of Prairie du Chien came about partly because of warfare between the Chippewas and the Sioux, and it attempted, unsuccessfully, to make peace between these two tribes. More important were boundary agreements that the various tribes made with the federal government. Each tribe agreed to live within specific boundaries, but the treaty gave the federal government the power to change those boundaries. Within a quarter of a century, the United States had taken possession of much of the area designated as Indian land.

Philadelphia artist O. J. Lewis painted this view of the 1825 Grand Council at Prairie du Chien. About 5,000 Indians representing eight different tribes attended the council, sponsored by the U.S. government to settle the boundary conflicts between the tribes.

THE INDIAN REMOVAL ACT AND THE TRAIL OF TEARS

As settlers pressed across the Appalachian Mountains and into the Ohio and Mississippi river valleys, tensions between these settlers and the Indians who lived in that land rose. After the Louisiana Purchase in 1803, the federal government began to draw up a plan for dealing with the Indians: The new Western territory could be used for the Indians, who would be given some of the "empty" land on the remote frontier.

In 1830, Congress made this plan official with the Indian Removal Act. This law allowed the government to offer the Indians land farther west in exchange for their Eastern territory. Although the law specifically required the Indians' consent to such trades, this provision was not enforced. Instead, over the next decade, tens of thousands of Indians were driven from their land. The Cherokee, Creek, Chocktaw, and Chickasaw Indians were driven to a new Indian Territory in what is now the state of Oklahoma. They were often forced to travel under terrible conditions, and thousands of them died from hunger, cold, and disease along the way. The Cherokees, who bitterly resisted their removal and were forced to march under Army guard, called the 1,700-mile route they traveled the Trail of Tears, a phrase that has come to symbolize the harshness of the removal policy.

In 1824, Congress created the Bureau of Indian Affairs as part of the War Department. The bureau became part of the Department of the Interior in 1849. In 1827, the bureau's director, Thomas L. McKenney (above), personally traveled to Mississippi to persuade the reluctant Choctaws to accept removal. This portrait appeared in McKenney's 1846 account of the trip.

This 1836 map, drawn by the U.S. Topographical Bureau, shows Indian Territory—the land "assigned to the Emigrant Indians." Large tracts in the southern part of the territory were set aside for the Five Civilized Tribes of the Southeast; smaller areas to the north were reserved for what remained of Great Lakes and Eastern tribes such as the Delaware and Sauk.

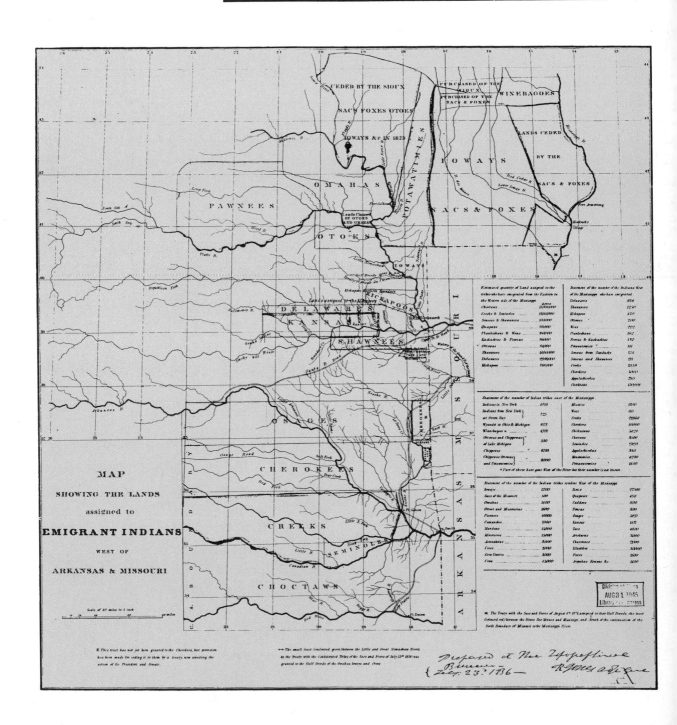

BLACK HAWK'S WAR

In the 1820s, the Sauk and Fox tribes, who traveled west to hunt during the winter, began to find when they returned each summer that settlers had taken over more and more of their land and property. Tension between the Indians and the settlers mounted for several years. Finally, in May 1832, Black Hawk and a group of only forty Indians encountered a force of almost 300 U. S. soldiers. In the battle that followed, Black Hawk won, to his great surprise.

Encouraged, the angry Indian chief led his people on a summer of violence against the settlers. Finally, in August, the Indians met a force of more than a thousand U. S. soldiers near the Mississippi River. Pinned between a warship on the river and the troops on land, Black Hawk's warriors were massacred. The Battle of Bad Axe, as this final battle was called, was the end of Black Hawk's short war.

Although Black Hawk (1767–1838; right) was the true leader of the Sauk and Fox tribes, the U.S. government negotiated a treaty with his rival, Keokuk. Black Hawk's refusal to obey this treaty—which would have forced him to move his village west of the Mississippi River—led to the war that has come to be known by his name.

In reality, Black Hawk's War was little more than a series of skirmishes, as militia and regular army troops chased Black Hawk and his band north along the Mississippi. The final battle (below) took place at the mouth of the Bad Axe River in Wisconsin on August 3, 1832, when about 1,300 militia and regular army troops trapped and overwhelmed Black Hawk and his handful of surviving followers.

WHITE SETTLERS AND INDIANS ON THE FRONTIER

The basic cause of the conflict between the Native Americans and the U. S. government was the steady flow of American settlers that kept pushing westward. Settlers set out to tame the land and establish farms, creating a way of life that could not exist side-by-side with the traditional Indian way of life. Many Americans considered the Indians savages, "wasting" the land they held because they used it only for hunting and minor agriculture. The settlers felt that they had a right—even a God-given duty—to put the land to "better" use by carving farms and communities out of the wilderness.

The Indians, whose livelihood and culture were threatened by these settlers, struck back when they could, capturing or killing isolated travelers and occasionally attacking smaller communities. Reports of these killings were often exaggerated among white settlers, which helped to keep alive the notion of Indian savagery. In fact, the struggle was a bitter and savage one on both sides, as the Indians fought to preserve, and the whites to expand, the way of life that each considered its right.

From the earliest colonial days, farms and settlements on the frontier faced the ever-present danger of Indian attack. Swift surprise attacks were the favorite tactic of most tribes. This 1901 print (above) illustrates an article by Woodrow Wilson, later president of the United States. In it, a colonial farmer, shot by Indians in the nearby woods, sprawls across his plow.

Taking captives from rival tribes—or white settlements—was a common practice among many Indian tribes. Accounts of the suffering endured by white captives made popular reading in early America, although these "captivity narratives" were almost always sensationalized and inaccurate. Shown here is the title page of one such narrative published in the aftermath of Black Hawk's War of 1832.

War and Pestilence!

TWO YOUNG LADIES TAKEN PRISONERS BY THE SAVAGES

The present year (1832) will be long remembered as a year of much human distress, and a peculiarly unfortunate one for the American nation ; for while many of her most populous cities have been visited by that dreadful disease, the CHOLERA, and to which great numbers have fallen victims, the merciless SAVAGES have been as industriously and fatally engaged in the work of human butchery, on the western frontiers ; where, while many have fallen victims to the bloody tomahawk, others have been conveyed away into captivity, to endure more protracted tortures of mind, as the following instances fully prove.---

JUST PUBLISHED,

An Interesting Narrative of the Captivity of

MISSES *FRANCIS* AND *ALMIRA HALL*,

Two respectable young females (sisters) of the ages of **16 and 18**,

Who were taken prisoners by the Savages at a Frontier Settlement, near Indian Creek, in May last, when fifteen of the inhabitants were barbarously murdered, among whom were the parents of the unfortunate females.

TO WHICH IS ADDED,

An affecting Narrative of the Captivity and Sufferings of

PHILIP BRIGDON,

A Kentuckian, who fell into the hands of the merciless Savages on their return to their settlement, three days after the Bloody Massacre.

Price of the Narrative 12 Cents.

☞ Please preserve this paper until called for.

INDIAN CULTURES AND DIFFERENT TERRAINS

This map, drawn by artist Seth Eastman in the 1850s, shows where the Indian tribes of North America lived in about 1650. Geography played an important part in shaping the lives of different tribes. The forested land of the East and along the West Coast, for example, offered plentiful trees for building, cooking, and heating—a resource that Indians living in the Plains and the Western desert did not have. While Northeastern tribes hunted deer and other small forest game, the Plains Indians hunted the mighty buffalo, and desert-dwelling Indians hunted and gathered small rodents, lizards, snakes—even insects—as well as seeds and berries.

In the dry region between the Rocky and Cascade mountains, inhabitants found plentiful food by fishing in the Columbia and other rivers. The tribes of the fertile Southeast and those in the hot, dry Southwest were skillful farmers, and led a much more settled way of life than did the hunters.

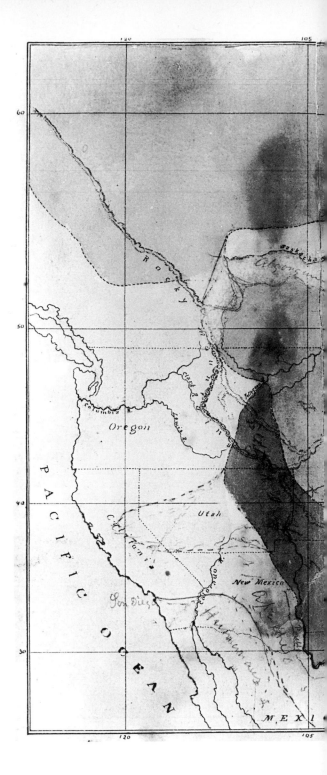

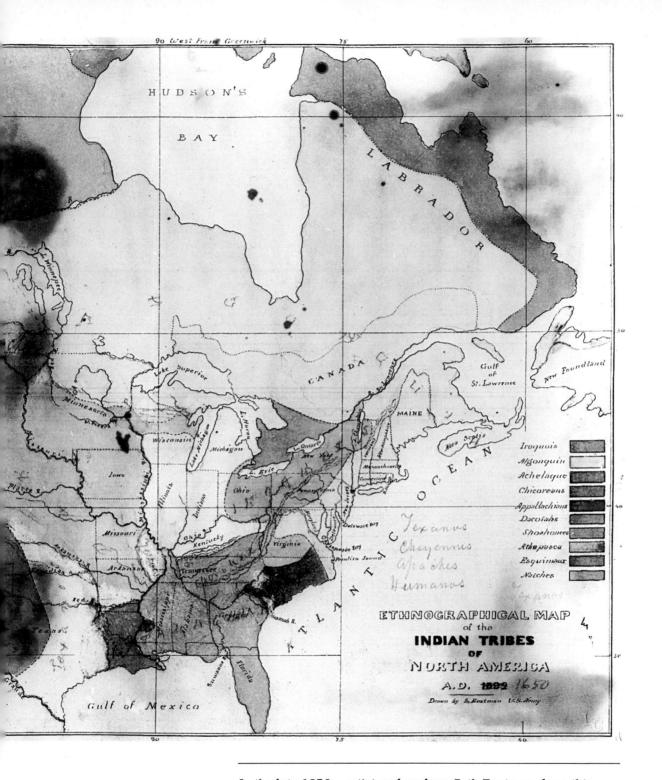

In the late 1850s, artist and explorer Seth Eastman drew this "Ethnographical" map of North America. It shows the distribution of Indian tribes in 1650—about midway between the time of the first European expeditions to the continent and the independence of the United States.

HENRY ROWE SCHOOLCRAFT

Henry Rowe Schoolcraft's many books about Indian history and culture, although colored by his strong belief that Indians should become Christian, are an important source of information about Indian life in the nineteenth century. Schoolcraft became an Indian agent in the Midwest in 1822, and remained there until 1841.

During this time he married an Ojibwa woman and became very knowledgeable about the Ojibwa tribe, as well as the other tribes that lived in the region he supervised. In the early 1840s he wrote a number of books, including a study of New York's Iroquois Indians and several books for a popular audience.

In 1849 he began his major work, a six-volume study of the nation's Indian tribes for the federal government. This work, *Historical and Statistical Information Respecting the History, Condition, & Prospects of the Indian Tribes of the United States*, was published between 1851 and 1857.

This engraving (opposite, top) from a sketch by Seth Eastman shows a Winnebago Indian village in what is now Wisconsin. Wigwams, made of animal skins stretched over wooden frames, were a common form of shelter. The conical shape of these structures differs from the triangular tipis favored by the Plains tribes farther west.

Corn was the major crop of farming tribes from New England to the Southwest. In this illustration (opposite, bottom), Indian women—probably from a Great Lakes tribe—frighten birds away from a field of ripening corn. In many tribes, women were responsible for raising crops while men hunted.

This engraving (below) from Henry R. Schoolcraft's History, Condition, & Prospects of the Indian Tribes of the United States *shows an Indian on Michigan's Upper Peninsula smelting iron ore from rocks. The ore would then be used to make tools. Few North American tribes practiced mining; most crafted tools traditionally—from bone, wood, or stone.*

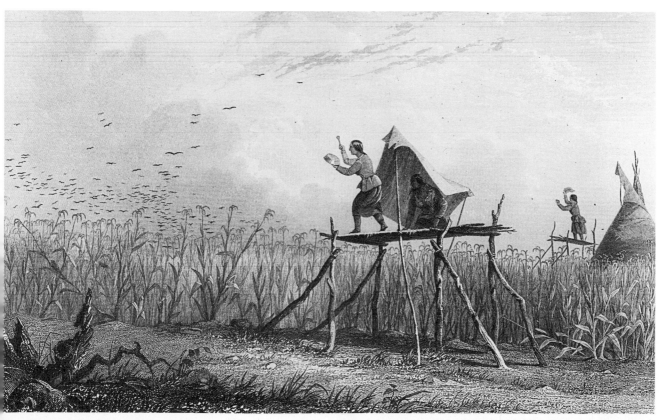

THE BUFFALO: LIVELIHOOD OF THE PLAINS INDIANS

For the Plains Indian tribes, the buffalo was essential to every part of life. Buffalo meat provided food, and their skin and bone provided clothing, blankets, and shelter (a tipi covered with buffalo hide was virtually weatherproof). Material from the buffalo was used to make everything from tools and snowshoes to water buckets and paintbrushes, and was also fashioned into weapons such as bow strings and arrowheads. The Indians had even devised ways to use buffalo parts for sport and pleasure. Stuffed buffalo skin could be made into balls or lacrosse nets, and bone could be made into dice.

Buffalo hunting was the primary activity of the Plains Indians, and a man was often judged by his skill in conquering this fearsome animal. White men gave the Indians guns and horses, two things that made hunting for buffalo considerably easier. But in the end, the effect of white men on buffalo hunting was disastrous for the Plains tribes. Farms and railroads interrupted the buffalo's migration patterns, and white settlers hunted buffalo—often merely for their hides—with such enthusiasm that they became almost extinct.

Swiss artist Peter Rindisbacher captures the fury of a traditional buffalo hunt in the 1820s (above), when buffalo were still plentiful on the Great Plains.

Many Plains tribes were nomadic—they moved from place to place with the seasons or to follow the buffalo herds. To carry their possessions, these tribes used their tipi poles as a triangular framework that could be lashed to dogs or horses, as shown in this illustration (right). French traders called the device the travois.

Plains tribes fought each other to win horses and captives, to avenge earlier raids, to prove their warriors' courage, or simply to drive rival tribes from favored hunting grounds. In this picture (above), Blackfoot Indians set fire to the grasslands around a Crow hunting camp, hoping to drive nearby buffalo onto Blackfoot land.

In this 1909 painting by Frederic Remington (left), Plains Indians try to lure buffalo away from the herd by draping themselves in buffalo hides to imitate the animals. The hunters are probably Sioux, because the painting is set in the Badlands of the Dakota Territory.

*The proud stance of this Sioux war chief reflects the tribe's repu-
tation as one of the fiercest Plains tribes. "Sioux" is a French vari-
ation of a Chippewa word for snake—the Chippewas considered
the Sioux their enemies. The Sioux are also known as the Dakota
Indians. In the Siouan language, the name "Dakota" means allies.*

PAINTING THE INDIANS OF THE PLAINS: CARL BODMER

In 1833, Swiss artist Carl Bodmer arrived in the United States with Prince Alexander Philip Maximilian of the small German state of Wied Nuwied. The prince had set out to make a serious scientific study of the American Plains region, and he brought the twenty-seven-year-old Bodmer along to make a visual record of their exploration. Bodmer produced some 400 works documenting their 3,000-mile journey. Among their many adventures, the explorers found themselves in the middle of an Indian battle, which Bodmer sketched as it unfolded.

Scholars appreciated Bodmer's useful attention to detail—although he did occasionally sacrifice accuracy to please his artistic sense. Overall, his works offer a beautiful and valuable glimpse of cultures that were about to disappear forever.

Many Plains tribes had secret societies of warriors who pledged to show special bravery in battle or on the hunt. These societies often took the names of animals, like the Dog Society of the Hidatsa tribe. Shown here (left), in a painting by Carl Bodmer, is a Hidatsa chief in the costume of the society.

This painting by Carl Bodmer (right) depicts an Indian mother and child. According to his notes, the mother was a Sioux while the child was an Assiniboin. The Assiniboins and the Sioux had once been allies, but they were enemies by the 1800s. The child may have been captured in a raid and adopted by the Sioux.

Ritual dance was an important part of the spiritual life of many North American tribes, especially those of the Great Plains. This Bodmer painting (below) depicts warriors of the Minnetaree tribe performing a scalp dance.

GEORGE CATLIN

American artist George Catlin began his career in Philadelphia, painting portraits. In the early 1830s, however, he became fascinated by Indians, whose culture and way of life were now threatened by President Andrew Jackson's policy of "removal," or pushing the Indians west to make room for more and more white settlers.

In 1832, Catlin made a 2,000-mile journey up the Missouri River to paint the Indians and their land before white settlement displaced them and changed their culture forever. By 1840, Catlin had created some 600 paintings. Known as the "Indian Gallery," these paintings were exhibited widely in both the United States and in Europe.

Catlin was not considered a great artist, and the speed of his work led to many inaccuracies. But as the first artist to undertake the task of preserving Native American life and culture, he provided a rare and valuable record through his work.

Northeastern and Plains Indians often used snowshoes in the winter months. This lithograph (opposite, top), modeled after a painting by George Catlin, shows a "snowshoe dance."

By the early 1800s, contact between whites and Indians was increasing—rarely to the Indians' benefit. This painting by George Catlin (opposite, bottom) is a "before and after" view of an Assiniboin chief named Anjonjon, who traveled east to Washington, D.C., in 1832. The artist portrays Anjonjon "after" as a ridiculously dressed dandy with bottles of whiskey in the pockets of his coat.

Members of three very different Indian groups are depicted in this nineteenth-century lithograph (below). At left is an Osage, a member of a tribe that originally lived in Missouri; at center is an Iroquois, a member of a powerful six-nation league in western New York; the woman at right belongs to the Pawnees, one of the major tribes of the Great Plains.

JOHN MIX STANLEY

Born in Canandaigua, New York, John
Mix Stanley was orphaned at fourteen.
He moved to Detroit when he was
twenty, worked as a sign-painter, and
began to study portraiture. In the
1840s, he went west, painting portraits and scenes of Indian life. In
1850, 150 of his paintings were dis-
played in the Smithsonian and later
stored there. He returned to the West
in 1853, this time as official artist for
a railway survey. In 1865, a fire in the
Smithsonian destroyed the wing con-
taining his paintings of Indians. Stanley was ruined. More of his paintings
were burned in an 1872 fire at P.T.
Barnum's American Museum. Stanley
died the same year.

Stanley made sketches and photographs while traveling, and only
painted when he returned to his stu-
dio in the East. In style, his work
shows a European influence and
reveals contradictory nineteenth-century attitudes about Indians as both
noble and terrifyingly barbaric.

Few of his paintings survive: The
Smithsonian's National Museum of
American Art has five. A handful of
others, including "On the Warpath,"
are reproduced in chromolithographs.

This lithograph, based on one of John Mix Stanley's paintings, depicts an Indian war party setting out on a raid. For many North American tribes, war was as much a way to prove the courage of the tribe's warriors as to settle differences with other groups.

INDIAN LAND FOR MONEY AND SUPPLIES

During the 1840s and 1850s, the United States spread quickly across the North American continent. In 1845, Texas joined the Union; in 1846, the United States gained title to the vast Oregon Country. And in 1848, Mexico surrendered the entire Southwest, from Texas to California, after the Mexican-American War.

Pioneers had begun settling Oregon in the early 1840s, and when gold was discovered in California in 1848 thousands of hopeful miners flooded there. There was no longer a Western frontier beyond which the government could push the Indians. Instead, the United States began to make treaties with the Indians that gave the federal government title to most of the western United States, while the Indians were squeezed into small protected areas known as reservations.

In the 1851 Treaty of Fort Laramie and the 1853 Treaty of Fort Atkinson, the Sioux, Cheyenne, Kiowa, Apache, and Comanche Indians, among other northern tribes, agreed to stop attacking the wagon trains of settlers traveling to Oregon and California. In exchange they were given a few million dollars and a clearly defined territory for each tribe. In the mid-1850s, tribes in Nebraska and parts of Kansas also signed away most of their land for money and reservations. At the Walla Walla Council of 1855, the Northwestern tribes signed away much of Oregon and Washington—a total of 60,000 square miles.

Isaac Stevens (1816–62; left), governor of the Washington Territory, was authorized to negotiate for the land claimed by the many tribes that lived along the Columbia River. At the Walla Walla Council in June 1855, representatives of five tribes agreed to cede almost 60,000 square miles in what is now Oregon and Washington to the U.S. government.

This map (below), credited to the Catholic missionary Father Pierre de Smet, shows the locations of the principal tribes of the Great Plains in 1851, the year the first Fort Laramie Treaty was signed.

THE

CONSTITUTION OF MINNESOTA,

IN THE

DAKOTA LANGUAGE,

TRANSLATED BY

STEPHEN R. RIGGS, A. M.

BY ORDER OF THE HAZLEWOOD REPUBLIC.

SMITHSONIAN INSTITUTION

BOSTON:
PRESS OF T. R. MARVIN & SON, 42 CONGRESS-ST.
1858.

Presbyterian missionary Stephen R. Riggs translated Minnesota's state constitution into the language of the Sioux Indians in 1858. The "Hazlewood Republic" mentioned on this title page (above) refers to the school Riggs founded to teach farming methods to the Sioux.

In order to convince Indians to leave their traditional homelands and settle on reservations, the U.S. government promised yearly "payments" of food and other goods. In this 1853 lithograph (below, top), government agents are distributing goods to the Assiniboins. That tribe was assigned a reservation between the Missouri and Yellowstone rivers by the Fort Laramie Treaty of 1851.

Many white trappers married Indian women, and their offspring often acted as translators and traders between the Indian and white worlds. This 1853 lithograph (below, bottom)—originally from a drawing by John Mix Stanley—shows a gathering of "half-breed" hunters camped along the Red River in Minnesota.

Part II: 1862–90
The Fight for the West

In this painting by Charles M. Russell, a Crow chief rides along a ridge, war lance ready. The Crow Indians provided many scouts and guides to the U.S. Army in its long campaign against the Sioux and other Plains Indians.

Once the Eastern Indians had been driven west of the Mississippi, the conflict between the Indians and the United States moved into the far West. Until the middle of the nineteenth century, the Western tribes had relatively little contact with white men. During the 1850s, many Western tribes had signed treaties ceding most of their territory. But it was not until the end of the Civil War that these treaties came to have any meaning. Then, with thousands of pioneers moving west, the Indians were pressured to move in order to open land to white settlement.

By 1870 most of the Western tribes, recognizing that they ultimately could never win against the larger and stronger force against them, had moved to reservations. Controlling the Indians was made easier because of divisions among the Indians themselves. Some believed that fighting was hopeless and argued for surrender, in order to preserve lives and perhaps some freedom. Others fought on, determined to resist the whites or to die trying.

In the end, many Indian tribes were defeated only with the help of Indian scouts and warriors hired by the army. As in the case of the Indians in the East, the Western Indians' failure to unite against their common enemy ultimately condemned them to defeat.

UNITED STATES HISTORY

Booth escaping after the murder of President Lincoln

1862 Two ironclad warships, the Union *Monitor* and the Confederate *Merrimac*, meet in the first sea battle of the Civil War, with neither ship winning a decisive victory.

1863 Lincoln issues the Emancipation Proclamation, freeing all slaves in seceding states.
•Ulysses S. Grant and his Union troops defeat Confederate forces at Vicksburg, Mississippi.

1865 Lincoln is shot and killed by actor and Southern patriot John Wilkes Booth at Ford's Theatre in Washington, D.C. Vice president Andrew Johnson is sworn in as president.
•Lee surrenders to Grant at Appomattox Courthouse in Virginia, ending the Civil War.

1867 After strong efforts by Secretary of State Seward, Congress ratifies the treaty to purchase Alaska from Russia and appropriates $7.2 million for payment. The value of the territory is unrecognized and Alaska is nicknamed "Seward's Folly."

1869 Congress adopts the Fifteenth Amendment, which gives black males the right to vote in both the North and South.
•The Wyoming Territory passes the first law in the United States giving women the right to vote.

NATIVE AMERICANS OF THE WEST

1862 A food shortage leads the Minnesota Sioux to begin the Santee Sioux Uprising; they destroy the Redwood agency and kill 800 settlers. Thirty-eight Sioux are hanged after the uprising is put down.

1864 Eight thousand Navajo Indians, driven to starvation by Kit Carson's troops, relocate to the Bosque Redondo Reservation in New Mexico, in what is known as the Long Walk.
•Colonel John Chivington leads 700 volunteers into Chief Black Kettle's camp on Sand Creek, where they massacre over 200 Cheyennes.

1866 Chief Red Cloud leads the Oglala Sioux and Cheyennes in an ambush near Fort Phil Kearny, defeating an eighty-man force under Captain William Fetterman. Known as the Fetterman Massacre, it marks the beginning of Red Cloud's War.

1868 A U.S. peace commission signs

Ely S. Parker

the Fort Laramie Treaty with the Sioux, designating territory in South Dakota west of the Missouri River as the Great Sioux Reservation.
•Missionary Pierre Jean de Smet travels alone into the Sioux stronghold on the Powder River and negotiates a treaty with Chief Sitting Bull.

1869 Ely S. Parker, chief of the Seneca, is appointed Commissioner of Indian Affairs by President Grant.

1872 Congress creates Yellowstone Park in Wyoming to help conserve the nation's endangered natural resources.
•Congress adopts the Amnesty Act, allowing Southerners to hold elective office again. Grant is reelected to the presidency over Democrat Horace Greeley.

1873 Gold becomes the U.S. monetary standard after Congress passes the Fourth Coinage Act and eliminates all silver currency.

The attack on the courthouse at Vicksburg, Mississippi

1874 Seventy blacks die when they riot and attack the courthouse at Vicksburg, Mississippi, after they learn of the dismissal a year before of a pro-black sheriff by whites.

1875 Congress passes the Civil Rights Act, guaranteeing blacks equal rights in public places.

1876 The presidential election ends in a deadlock, with Democrat Samuel Tilden receiving about 250,000 more popular votes than his Republican opponent, Rutherford B. Hayes. Returns from four states are in dispute.
•The National League of Baseball is organized. Boston beats Philadelphia, six to five, in the League's first official game.

1871 The House of Representatives passes the Indian Appropriation Act, which refuses to acknowledge any tribe as an independent nation.

1872 The Modoc War begins in California. The Modoc Indians successfully fight off U.S. military attacks for five months before they are defeated and exiled into Indian Territory.

1874 General Philip Sheridan heads a campaign, known as the Red River War, against those Kiowa, Comanche, and Cheyenne tribes attempting to leave their reservations and move west.

1876 A band of Sioux and Cheyenne warriors, led by Crazy Horse and Chief Sitting Bull, wipe out General George Custer and his 200 soldiers at the Battle of Little Bighorn in Montana.
•General Nelson Appleton Miles pursues Crazy Horse and Sitting Bull through the winter, driving Sitting Bull into exile in Canada.

1877 Military attempts to subdue "non-treaty" Nez Perces who refuse to live on the reservation at Clearwater, Idaho, result in the Nez Perce War of 1877.

General Miles meets Sitting Bull

UNITED STATES HISTORY

1878 The Democrats gain control of both houses of Congress for the first time since 1858.
•Congress passes the Bland-Allison Act, which requires the government to buy at least $2 million worth of silver each month to be minted into coins.

1879 Congress passes an act allowing women lawyers to argue before the Supreme Court.

1880 Republicans James A. Garfield and Chester A. Arthur win the national election for president and vice president.
•Wabash, Indiana, becomes the first town to be lit completely by electric light.

1881 Former school teacher and Civil War nurse Clara Barton organizes the American Red Cross.

1882 Overriding President Arthur's

A leaflet from the Red Cross

veto, Congress passes the Chinese Exclusion Act, prohibiting Chinese laborers from entering the U.S. for ten years.
•The U.S. and Korea sign a treaty of friendship and commerce.

•Labor strikes by the Amalgamated Association of Iron and Steel Workers disrupt the railroad industry for several weeks.

1883 Congress passes the Pendleton Act in reaction

NATIVE AMERICANS OF THE WEST

1878 The Bannock War breaks out in Idaho over treaty violations; the Indians turn themselves in three years later.

1879 Ute Indians in Colorado are forced to move to Utah after their uprising is put down by U.S. troops.

1881 Reformer Helen Hunt Jackson exposes government mistreatment of the Indians in her book titled *A Century of Dishonor*. The Department of the Interior hires her to investigate Indian conditions in California.

1886 General George S. Crook persuades Geronimo and his Apache warriors to

Helen Hunt Jackson

meet with him at the Canyon de Los Embudos in the Sierra Madres in Mexico. Geronimo agrees to end the raids and relocate the Apaches to reservations, providing they are reunited with their families held at Ft. Marion, Florida.

1887 The Dawes Severalty Act proposes dividing reservation lands into individual family units, in order to reduce tribal connections.

to President Garfield's assassination. The law establishes a three-person Civil Service Commission in an attempt to end political patronage.
•Indiscriminate tree-cutting and wasteful farming methods lead to severe flooding of the Ohio River. Damage to the area costs millions.

1884 The Supreme Court declares it a federal offense to attempt to interfere with a person's right to vote. The case was brought by Southern blacks who had been prevented from voting by the Ku Klux Klan.

The Washington Monument

1885 The Washington Monument is dedicated in the nation's capital.

1886 The Statue of Liberty is dedicated in New York harbor.

1888 Benjamin Harrison is elected president.
•A yellow fever epidemic kills 400 people in Jacksonville, Florida.
•Designer Phillip Pratt demonstrates the first electric automobile—a tricycle powered by batteries.
•Congress estab-lishes the U.S. Department of Labor to deal with issues regarding labor and management.

1890 States continue to pass anti-trust laws leading Congress to pass the Sherman Anti-Trust Act.
•The National Women's Suffrage Association forms in an effort to win women the right to vote in national elections.

The aftermath of Wounded Knee

•Geronimo and his warriors agree to conditional surrender for the second time.

1889 Wovoka, a Paiute visionary also known as Jack Wilson, starts the Ghost Dance. This religious movement seeks to reunite Native Americans with their dead ancestors and with the land through ritual and dancing.
•The U.S. government officially opens the Indian Territory to settlers. The Territory had previously been protected land, home to 75,000 Indians from twenty-two tribes.

1890 Tensions between whites and Indians, resulting from the popularity of the Ghost Dance movement, leads to the massacre at Wounded Knee, South Dakota. At least 250 Indians are killed, and fifty more wounded; two-thirds of the casualties are women and children.

THE SANTEE UPRISING

In August 1862, the Santee Sioux of Minnesota launched a terrible attack on white settlers. The uprising began simply enough: A group of four braves came upon a nest of eggs that belonged to a nearby farm, and one wanted to take them. Another warned him not to take something that obviously belonged to a white man. They fell to arguing, and ended up boasting to each other that they weren't afraid of whites. To prove themselves, they killed the farmer, his family, and his neighbors—five people in all.

That night the tribal chiefs debated about whether to turn the murderers in or to launch an all-out attack. Despite Chief Little Crow's warning that they would never win, the Santees were angry about the reservation system and their treatment by the government, and they decided to attack. Before the Indians were finally defeated a month later, 800 whites had been killed. Almost 400 Indians were taken prisoner in the final battle, and more than 300 of these were sentenced to death. President Abraham Lincoln intervened, however, and reduced the number who were actually hanged to thirty-eight.

Chief Little Crow farmed, wore store-bought clothes, and even joined the Episcopal Church. But when the Santee Sioux uprising broke out in 1862, the sixty-year-old chief reluctantly agreed to take part. He survived the fighting only to be shot and killed in a farmer's field in 1863.

Thirty-eight Santee Sioux were hanged at Mankato, Minnesota, on December 26, 1863, as shown in this engraving. The numbers would have been much higher if President Abraham Lincoln hadn't ordered many sentences overturned, but at least one of the Indians was executed due to mistaken identity.

THE PEACE COMMISSION

After the end of the Civil War, settlers once again began to flood into the West. With the help of railroads, they traveled in even greater numbers than before, and it soon became impossible to ignore the growing hostility of the Plains tribes. Accordingly, Congress established a Peace Commission to meet with Indians, to "remove the causes of war. . .and establish a system for civilizing the tribes." In 1867 the Peace Commissioners set out toward southern Kansas. There, in a place called Medicine Lodge, they met with representatives of the Cheyenne, Comanche, Arapaho, and other hostile tribes. The government promised food, clothes, and housing if the Indians would leave Kansas and move to reservations south of the Arkansas River. Chief Black Kettle of the Cheyenne tribe helped win the doubtful Indians over to the cause of peace, and the treaty was signed. Sadly, neither side kept the promises it had made, and only a year later hostilities were again raging.

This engraving shows an Indian speaking at one of the meetings that led to the 1867 Medicine Lodge Treaty. The treaty, signed at Medicine Lodge, Kansas, was the keystone of the U.S. Government's "Peace Policy."

RED CLOUD'S WAR

When gold was discovered in Montana in 1863, hopeful miners began pouring into the gold fields along the new Bozeman Trail, through prime Oglala Sioux hunting territory. Angered, the Sioux, led by Red Cloud and several other chiefs, attacked travelers along the trail relentlessly. Finally, in 1866, a peace council was arranged at Fort Laramie. Just as the Sioux were about to sign a treaty permitting travelers to use the trail, Colonel Henry Carrington arrived with a large force of soldiers to secure the trail. Red Cloud and several other chiefs were wise enough to know that where there were forts and soldiers, Indian hunting could not continue for long, treaty or not. Indignant, the Indian leaders stormed out of the council.

Although the remaining Sioux chiefs signed the treaty, Red Cloud launched a campaign against Carrington's forces. In December of that year, Crazy Horse and his warriors drew Captain William Fetterman and his men into a perfect trap, killing all eighty soldiers. Red Cloud's War was so effective that the United States government eventually agreed to the Sioux chief's demands and abandoned the forts along the trail. In return, Red Cloud signed the Fort Laramie Treaty of 1868, agreeing to resettle the Sioux on the Great Sioux Reservation in Dakota Territory. It was the first—and last—time that a Western tribe won concessions from the government.

Red Cloud (above, at right) was photographed with American Horse, another Sioux leader, in 1891. An able war leader, Red Cloud was described by an army officer as being "as full of action as a tiger." After the conflict over the Bozeman Trail, he worked peacefully to promote the cause of his people until his death in 1909.

In September 1868, shortly after the end of Red Cloud's War, Cheyennes in Colorado trapped fifty U.S. soldiers on a tiny island in the Arikara River. Chief Roman Nose led charge after charge against the island's defenders, as depicted in this painting (right), but after nine days of combat another army unit arrived and drove off the Cheyennes.

R.F. Zogbaum

After the Fort Laramie Treaty of 1868 ended the conflict over the Bozeman Trail, Red Cloud traveled east. In 1870, he gave a historic speech at New York City's Cooper Union, in which he asked the American public for help in winning fair treatment for the Indians. He also attended a reception at the White House where he met President Grant, as shown in this engraving (right).

In the vast expanse of the Great Plains, cavalry units often had an advantage over the slower-moving infantry. This newspaper engraving (left) shows a battle between Cheyenne warriors and the U.S. 7th Cavalry near Fort Larned in Kansas in 1867.

SURPRISE ATTACKS AND MASSACRES

Hopes for peace between the Indians and the white settlers on the Great Plains were dashed both by Indian and by white treachery. Although Indian massacres like the Santee uprising of 1862 were more widely reported, there were several notable massacres of Indians by whites.

In 1864, at Sand Creek in eastern Colorado, U.S. Colonel John Chivington led an unprovoked attack on a group of Cheyennes led by Black Kettle and White Antelope, who had gone quietly where they were told to go after meeting in a peace council only two months before. In a surprise attack at dawn, as many as 200 Cheyennes, most of them women and children, were killed. All had believed they were under U.S. Army protection.

Black Kettle survived, but only to face another grisly massacre. The Battle of Washita, in November 1868, was led by George Custer and the U.S. 7th Cavalry in retaliation for Cheyenne raids in Kansas. This time Black Kettle himself died, alongside forty other Cheyennes, many of them women and children.

On November 27, 1868, soldiers commanded by Lieutenant Colonel George Custer stormed the village of Cheyenne chief Black Kettle along the Washita River (shown below). Black Kettle, who wanted peace, had already survived the brutal Sand Creek massacre of 1864; this time he was killed. The attack came in retaliation for Cheyenne raids on nearby white settlements.

THE MODOC WAR

From November 1872 to June 1873, the Modoc Indians, a tribe from northern California, led a war to win back their traditional homeland. Although the Modocs had agreed in 1864 to leave their native territory and resettle on a reservation in Oregon, they were unhappy living with the other tribes there, and returned to California a year later under Captain Jack, leader of the Kientapoos. An uneasy peace between the Modocs and the white settlers in the area lasted until 1872, when the army finally tried to root the Modocs out.

The Modocs stood their ground at Lake Tule, where spectacular lava formations offered a fine defensive position. In January 1873, fifty Modoc warriors fought off some 400 soldiers in the Battle of Jack's Stronghold. The Modocs continued to hold their position until mid-May, when disagreements led most of the Indians to leave their hiding place. By the end of the month, the army had rounded up the scattered groups. Captain Jack was captured on June 1, and the Modoc War was over.

Modoc leader Kintpuash (c. 1838–73; above) was nicknamed "Captain Jack" because of his habit of wearing military medals. His tribe had dwindled to about 250 people, only eighty of them capable of acting as warriors, when the Modoc War of 1872 erupted.

It took about 1,000 troops, over 100 of whom were killed or wounded, to drive the Modocs from the lava beds of northern California. Among the casualties was General E. S. Canby, shot by Kintpuash (right) while attempting to negotiate an end to the conflict. After hearing of the murder, General-in-Chief William Sherman wrote to President Grant, "You will be fully justified in utter extermination [of the Modocs]."

INDIANS AND THE "IRON HORSE"

In the years after the Civil War, few things were more threatening to Indians of the American West than the railroads that raced across the Western United States. The "Iron Horse," as the Indians christened the locomotive, brought ever greater numbers of white settlers right through the middle of Indian Territory. The settlers brought west by the railroads invaded the land Indians thought they had secured by treaty and disturbed Indian life in profound ways. Both the railroads and the farms of the settlers violated Indian hunting grounds and interrupted the vital migrations of buffalo.

Indians, especially the Cheyennes and Sioux, struck back in every way they could. They assaulted railroad crews, tore up tracks, and even attacked trains. In the end, however, they were no match for the relentless industrial energy of the United States.

In this fanciful lithograph (right), Indians pry apart the rails of the Union Pacific Railroad's roadbed as a train approaches. Such outright attacks were rare, but Indians did occasionally raid the camps of tracklaying crews.

The rapid advance of the railroad in the late 1800s spelled doom for the buffalo—and when the buffalo were gone, so was the centuries-old way of life of the Plains Indians. Professional and sport hunters reduced the buffalo population from about 15 million before the Civil War to a few thousand by 1890. In this painting (right), a buffalo herd blocks a train, and the passengers wile away the delay by shooting at the animals.

THE WAR FOR
THE BLACK HILLS

Pressure on the northern Plains tribes did not let up even after Red Cloud signed the 1868 Treaty of Fort Laramie. As usual, both sides quickly broke the treaty. The Indians continued to raid white settlements, and settlers and soldiers continued to push into Sioux territory around the Bozeman Trail. Then, in 1874, gold was discovered in the Black Hills region, a place that was sacred to the Sioux. Thousands of miners soon arrived, with complete disregard for the promises that had been made to the Sioux. When the Sioux refused to sell the Black Hills, the government commanded them to resettle on the reservation nearby or be hunted down.

The War for the Black Hills began in March 1876, when General George Crook sent his cavalry against a camp of Cheyennes and Oglala Sioux in the Battle of Powder River. The army was eventually forced to withdraw. In June, a united Indian force of nearly a thousand warriors, led by Sitting Bull and Crazy Horse, faced the army again in the Battle of Rosebud Creek. Although this time the Indians withdrew, they cut Crook off from the rest of the army. Following that battle, the Indian force doubled in size. Settled in a camp along a stream they called Greasy Grass, they prepared for a final showdown.

The Black Hills, in what is now South Dakota, are one of the few striking natural landmarks on the otherwise featureless Great Plains. The region had great religious significance for the Sioux, who called the hills Paha Sapa ("sacred ground"). In addition, they also prized the hills as a source of wood and game. This engraving, taken from a painting by Albert Bierstadt, gives a sense of the region's beauty.

In this Frederic Remington engraving (left), titled "A Reconnaissance," an army officer hears a report from an Indian scout. These scouts, recruited from friendly tribes such as the Crows on the Plains and some of the Apache groups in the Southwest, played a vital part in the army's many campaigns against "hostile" tribes.

This newspaper illustration (opposite, top) depicts the battle along the Rosebud River in southern Montana in which Sioux and Cheyennes, led by Crazy Horse, fought U.S. troops under General George Crook. After two hours of battle, Crook's men were forced to retreat. This Indian victory was followed by an even greater triumph along the nearby Little Bighorn River.

Scenes of mounted combat (opposite, bottom) were rare during the Indian Wars. Cavalrymen almost never carried their heavy, cumbersome swords on campaign, and both Indians and soldiers preferred firearms.

The army learned to use Indian methods in its wars in the West. Below, the 5th Cavalry adopts the traditional travois of the Plains Indians as an ambulance for a trooper wounded in one of the battles that followed the 7th Cavalry's defeat at the Battle of Little Bighorn in 1876.

THE BATTLE OF LITTLE BIGHORN

The army's name for the area the Indians called Greasy Grass was Little Bighorn. The officers prepared to attack the Indian camp there from two directions. George Custer, who had led the attack at the Washita River in 1868, was to position the 600 men of the 7th Cavalry south of the Indian encampment, while another force led by General Alfred Terry and Colonel John Gibbon took up a position north of the Indians. Custer arrived near the Indian camp on June 25, 1876. Fearing that the Indians would scatter if they discovered his presence, he decided to attack before Terry and Gibbon's force was in place.

He had not determined where the Indian camp was, however, nor did he know the lay of the land. He divided his troops into several parts, and he himself led a group of 210 men north. They were quickly trapped on a ridge, attacked from the south by the Hunkpapa Sioux leader Gall and the Cheyenne leader Lame White Man, while Crazy Horse led the Oglala Sioux in an attack from the north. Within an hour, Custer and every one of his men had been killed. Custer's Last Stand, as the Battle of Little Bighorn is also known, was the most famous Indian victory in the Western wars.

Artists have produced many depictions of the Battle of Little Bighorn—despite the fact that none of the white participants survived to describe it. Like most of these depictions, this lithograph shows General George Custer as one of the last men standing. But according to Indian accounts of the battle—and the location of his corpse—Custer was among the first men killed.

After graduating last in his class from West Point, Custer (left) won fame and a quick promotion by leading several brave (but not particularly skillful) cavalry charges in the Civil War. His commander described him as "a reckless, gallant boy."

Weeks before the Battle of Little Bighorn, Sitting Bull (c. 1831–90; opposite, bottom) predicted a great Indian victory; after performing a painful ritual called the Sun Dance, he had a vision of bluecoated soldiers falling upside down into the Sioux camp. Whites considered Sitting Bull the "commander" of the Sioux and the Cheyennes, but in fact he was more of a statesman and spiritual leader. He preferred to leave the fighting to Crazy Horse and other able warriors.

After the army's defeat at Little Bighorn, General Nelson Miles arrived in the West to hunt down the "hostile" bands of Sitting Bull and Crazy Horse. In October 1876, Miles and Sitting Bull met under a white flag (below), but the chief refused Miles's demand that he and his band surrender and go to a reservation.

THE NEZ PERCE WARS

In 1863, gold was discovered in the Clearwater River area of Idaho, which had been until that time the exclusive territory of the Nez Perce Indians. One part of the tribe, led by Chief Joseph and later by his son, refused to surrender their land. They were allowed to remain in the Wallowa Valley for another decade. But by the mid-1870s, white settlers were pressing the government to force the Nez Perces off this land and open it for settlement. This time, seeing that resistance would be futile, the Nez Perces left, bitterly, in the spring of 1877.

As they left, angry warriors killed several white settlers. The army pursued, and the Nez Perces decided to make a dramatic escape to seek protection from the northern Plains tribes. Over the next three months, a group of 800 Nez Perce men, women, and children made a grueling 1,700-mile march, pursued by 700 soldiers. Eventually they decided to head for Canada, where Sitting Bull and the Sioux had escaped. Forty miles short of the Canadian border, the army caught up with them. While 300 Indians managed to escape to Canada, Chief Joseph and the remaining tribe members surrendered on October 5th.

While their dramatic journey won them the sympathy of the nation, and their leaders' military skill had won them the praise of the army, the Nez Perces were never allowed to return to their land.

The bravery and skill of Chief Joseph (c. 1840–1904; right) in leading 800 Nez Perces on a 1,700-mile journey from Oregon to northern Montana won him the grudging admiration of the U.S. Army; his moving surrender speech brought him fame throughout the nation.

In this Frederic Remington print (below), a cavalry unit fords a stream during the army's pursuit of the Nez Perces. The campaign was an embarrassment to the army—it finally took thousands of troops, and several artillery pieces, to block Chief Joseph's escape into Canada, and the freezing weather of the Bear Paw mountains did as much to halt the Nez Perces as the army.

THE APACHE WARS

The battle to subdue the Apaches began in 1861, when an army lieutenant demanded the return of a white boy the Chiricahua Apaches had taken hostage. The following struggle, led by the Apache chief Cochise, resulted in ten years of raids and counterraids. An unprovoked massacre of as many as 150 Apaches in 1871 led to a peace council in which Cochise finally surrendered. Still, thousands of other Apaches fought on.

Beginning in the winter of 1872, the army waged the Tonto Basin campaign, a determined effort to round up the remaining Apaches. By the spring of 1873, some 6,000 Apaches had agreed to relocate to a reservation. But some Chiricahua Apaches continued to resist reservation life. The great Apache Victorio led a band of 150 warriors, attacking soldiers and settlers. They eluded the army for a year before Victorio was killed in 1880.

The final Apache war was waged by another legendary Apache leader, Geronimo. Geronimo and a small band of Apaches had fled the reservation once, only to be hunted down in Mexico's Sierra Madres in 1883. But two years later, in 1885, he and some 130 followers made another break. Terrorizing settlers wherever they went, Geronimo and his warriors held out for more than a year. Finally, in despair at the news that the rest of his tribe had been taken from Arizona to Florida, Geronimo surrendered at Skeleton Canyon on September 4, 1886. The Apache Wars were over.

Geronimo (far right) was photographed with three warriors of the Chiricahua Apache band in 1886. The fierce and hardy Apaches could be fought only by soldiers who adapted to the harsh conditions of the Southwestern desert—like General George Crook, who replaced his troops' horses with tougher, more efficient mules.

C. S. Fly, an enterprising Arizona photographer, took this dramatic shot (below) of Geronimo and his warriors in Mexico's Sierra Madre mountains. Apache bands often operated in the mountains and deserts of northern Mexico, sometimes making it necessary for U.S. troops to cross the border in pursuit.

HARPER'S WEEKLY.
A JOURNAL OF CIVILIZATION.

Vol. XXX.—No. 1516.
Copyright, 1886, by Harper & Brothers.

NEW YORK, SATURDAY, JANUARY 9, 1886.

TEN CENTS A COPY.
$4.00 PER YEAR, IN ADVANCE.

THE APACHE WAR—INDIAN SCOUTS ON GERONIMO'S TRAIL.—Drawn by Frederic Remington.—[See Page 23.]

This remarkable photograph (above) shows Geronimo (third from left) and General George Crook (third from right) in Canyon de los Embudos in the Sierra Madres of Mexico in March 1886. Crook, an honest soldier respected by the Apaches, talked Geronimo and his band into surrendering, but Geronimo escaped after Crooks's successor, General Nelson Miles, broke the surrender terms.

Army patrols relied on Indian scouts from friendly Apache tribes to help them follow Geronimo's trail. This 1886 engraving (opposite), Frederic Remington's first signed picture for Harper's Weekly, shows scouts leading a patrol in search of Geronimo along the Mexican border.

Geronimo adopted some of the white way of life in his last years. He joined the Dutch Reformed Church, kept a farm, and rode in President Theodore Roosevelt's inaugural parade. In this 1908 photograph (right), taken a year before his death, the top-hatted chief—once the terror of Arizona and northern Mexico—poses at the wheel of a car.

WOUNDED KNEE

In the late 1880s, the Sioux, confined on reservations and forced to farm land too poor to support them, found hope in a new religion called the Ghost Dance, spread by a Paiute Indian named Wovoka. Wovoka promised believers a future world in which the Indians could return to their lands and traditional ways. Although Wovoka himself taught that the way to this new world was never to fight, the Sioux decided that if they fought against their oppressors the day of freedom would come sooner.

As Ghost Dance ceremonies among the Sioux began to sound more and more violent, government officials on the Sioux reservations became worried. In the fall of 1890 they finally brought in troops to stop the dances. That December, the army sent Indian policemen to arrest the legendary Sioux chief, Sitting Bull; his people resisted, and the chief was killed. The army then tried to arrest another Sioux leader named Big Foot. They found him, with about 350 people, near Wounded Knee Creek on December 28. Infantry attempted to disarm the Sioux, who resisted. When one Indian rifle accidentally discharged, the soldiers opened fire. Within an hour, at least 250 Indians had been killed, many of them women and children. Although it took until January 15th for General Nelson Miles to talk the remaining Sioux into surrendering, Wounded Knee was the end of the fighting. After more than a century, the Indians were finally defeated.

The origins of the Ghost Dance were peaceful, but some members of Plains tribes, bitter over their treatment by the government, gave the movement violent overtones. Still, Indian agents overreacted when they saw scenes of wild dancing like the one in this engraving (right) from a British newspaper. Agents at the South Dakota reservations nervously cabled Washington to send troops, making violence almost inevitable.

Like many other depictions of incidents in the Indian wars, this lithograph (below), titled "The Capture and Death of Sitting Bull," is completely inaccurate. Sitting Bull was actually arrested by thirty-three Indian policemen in his cabin at the Standing Rock Indian Agency. When he refused to surrender, a scuffle broke out, followed by gunfire. When the brief, one-sided fight was over, Sitting Bull and his young nephew Crow Foot were dead.

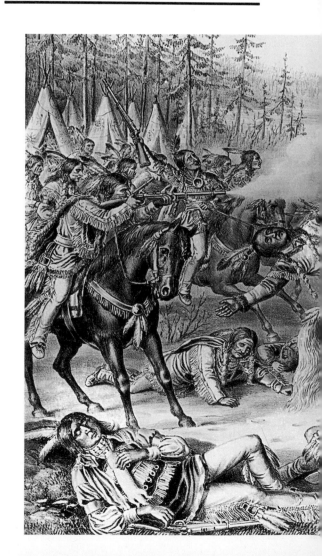

Buried of the Dead
at the Battle of Wounded Knee S.D.

NorthWestern Photo Co
Chadron Neb.

While inaccurate in most ways, this Frederic Remington print (opposite, top) does show the sudden and confused nature of the "fight" at Wounded Knee. Most of the army's casualties were soldiers caught in their fellow soldiers' crossfire. Most of the hundreds of Indian deaths were caused not by rifle fire but by cannons firing explosive shells from the ridge above Wounded Knee Creek.

A few days after the tragedy at Wounded Knee Creek, mass graves were hacked into the frozen South Dakota soil. As the photograph here (opposite, bottom) shows, the bodies of 200 to 300 Sioux—the exact number isn't known—were unceremoniously dumped into the graves while soldiers and civilians looked on.

The Pine Ridge Reservation (below) looks peaceful in this 1891 photo by local photographer John Grabill. The camera only hints at the tragedy of the scene—a people uprooted from their homes, defeated in battle, and forced to make a new life in a harsh and unfamiliar world.

Resource Guide

Key to picture positions: (T) top, (C) center, (B) bottom; and in combinations: (TL) top left, (TC) top center, (TR) top right, (BL) bottom left, (BC) bottom center, (BR) bottom right.

Key to picture locations within the Library of Congress collections (and where available, photo negative numbers): P - Prints and Photographs; HABS -

Historical American Buildings Survey (div. of Prints and Photographs); R - Rare Book Division; G - General Collections; MSS - Manuscript Division; G&M - Geography and Map Division.

PICTURES IN THIS VOLUME

2-3 Camp, G **4-5** Utensils, G **6-7** Warrior, P **8-9** Map, G

Part I: **10-11**, Sequoya, P **12-13** TL, church, P, USZ62-15059; BL, Little Turtle, P; BR, Village, P, USZ62-53566 **14-15** BL, meeting, P, USZ62-32586; TR, title page, G **16-17** C, serpent mound, P, USZ62-049402 **18-19** TL, medicine man, P, USZ62-2182; TR, rock painting, P, USZ62-049642; BR, cliff dwellings, P, USZ62-101891 **20-21** TR, fort, G; BR, surrender, G **22-23** TL, battle, G; TR, Wayne, G; BR, Little Turtle, P **24-25** BC, Tippecanoe, G; TR, Tenskwatawa, P, USZ62-31690 **26-27** TL, Tecumseh, P, USZ62-48755; BL, cartoon, P; TR, death, P **28-29** BL, map, G&M; TR, McIntosh, P; BR, Fort Mims, P, USZ62-36279 **30-31** C, Prairie du Chien, P **32-33** TL, McKenney P, USZ62-30703; TR, map, G&M **34-35** BC, boat, P, USZ62-90; TR, Black Hawk, P **36-37** TL, farmer, R; TR, title page, P, USZ62-43902 **38-39** C, map, G&M **40-41** BL, mining, P, US62-9307; TR, wigwam, P, USZ62-19901; BR, birds, P, USZ62-2735 **42-43** TC, buffalo, G; BR, hunting, P, USA7-34113 **44-45** TL, fire, G; BL, buffalo hides, P, D4-90473; TR, war chief, G **46-47** TL, dog dance, G; C, scalp dance, G; TR, mother and child, G **48-49** BL, three Indians, P; TR, dance, G; BR, Anjonjon, P **50-51** TL, Stevens, P, USZ62-19726; BC, map, G&M **52-53** TL,

title page, R; TC, agents, P, USZ62-060006; BC, hunters, P, USZ62-8178

Part II: **54-55**, Indian, G **56-57** TL, Booth, P, USZ6214142; BL, Parker, P, USZ62-14456; TR, courthouse, G; BR, Miles, P, USZ62-11123 **58-59** TL, Red Cross, G; BL, Jackson, G; TR, monument, G; BR, Wounded Knee, G **60-61** C, war party, G **62-63** TL, Little Crow, P, USZ61-83; BR, hanging, P, USZ62-37940 **64-65** C, meeting, G **66-67** TL, Red Cloud, P, USZ62-11568; TR, fighting, G **68-69** TC, battle, P; BC, reception, P **70-71** C, village, P, USZ62-44083 **72-73** TL, Kintpuash, G; TR, Modoc War, G **74-75** BC, railroad, P; TR, buffalo, P, USZ62-44079 **76-77** C, Black Hills, R **78-79** TL, scout, G; BL, travois, G; TR, Rosebud River, P, USZ6254652; BR, mounted combat, P, USZ62-14070 **80-81** C, Little Bighorn, G **82-83** TL, Custer, P, USZ62-48894; BL, Chief Joseph, P, USZ62-069167; C, cavalry, G **84-85** BC, Miles, P, USZ62-4164; TR, Sitting Bull, P, USZ62-49148 **86-87** BC, warriors, P, USZ62-20043; TR, Geronimo, P, USZ62-35647 **88-89** TL, newspaper, G; TR, car, P, USZ62-11481; BR, Crook, P, USZ62-11624 **90-91** BC, capture, P, USZ62-196; TR, dancing, P, USZ62-051120 **92-93** TL, graves, P, USZ62-44458; BL, Wounded Knee, P, USZ62-26192; BR, Pine Ridge, P, USZ62-19725

SUGGESTED READING

DANIEL, CLIFTON. *Chronicle of America.* New York: Prentice Hall, 1989.

JOSEPHY, ALVIN M., JR. *The World Almanac of the American West.* New York: Pharos Books, 1986.

MORRISON, SAMUEL E. *The Oxford History of the American People.* New York: Oxford University Press, 1965.

WARDWELL, LELIA. *The Native American Experience.* New York: Facts on File, 1990.

WILLS, CHARLES. *The Battle of Little Bighorn.* New York: Silver Burdett, 1991.

Index

Page numbers in *italics* indicate illustrations